THE LIVES OF MINIBEASTS

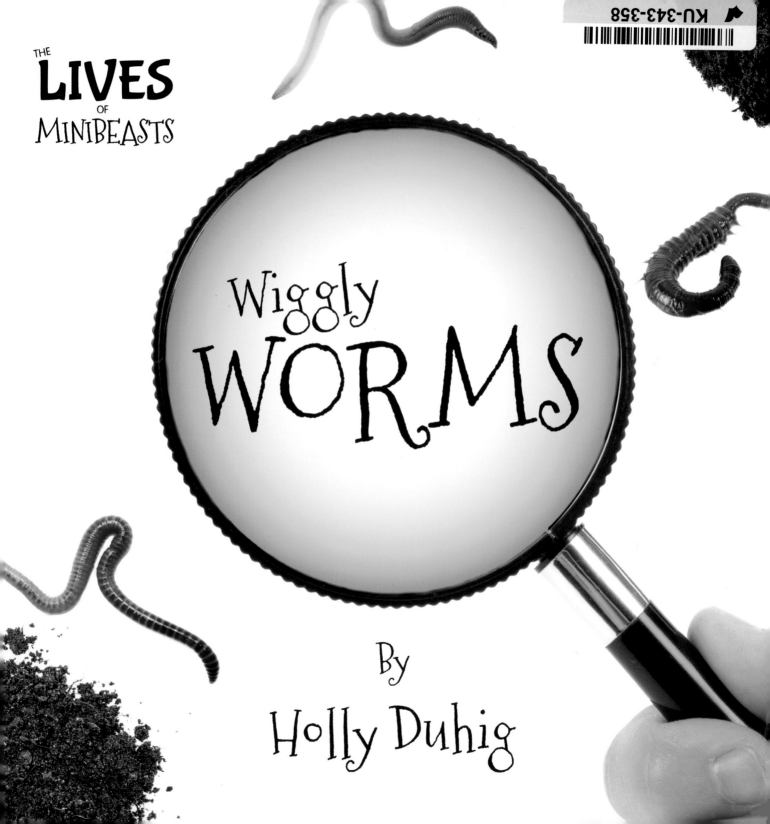

Wiggly WORMS

By Holly Duhig

©2017
Book Life
King's Lynn
Norfolk PE30 4LS

ISBN: 978-1-78637-188-1

Written by:
Holly Duhig

Edited by:
Charlie Ogden

Designed by:
Danielle Jones

A catalogue record for this book
is available from the British Library

Photo Credits

Abbreviations: l-left, r-right, b-bottom, t-top, c-centre, m-middle.

Cover & throughout – jps, kzww, Sarah2, Foto2rich, MRAORAOR, hsagencia, schankz, HHelene, Pan Xunbin, GongTo, Feng Yu, xpix. 2–Patila. 3–Maryna Pleshkun. 4–Pavel Hlystov. 6–Alexander Sviridov. 7–Africa Studio. 8–By Andreas th Andreas Thomsen (Own work) [CC BY-SA 3.0 (http://creativecommons.org/licenses/by-sa/3.0)], via Wikimedia Commons. 9–By Clive A. Edwards, The Ohio State University, Columbus. (United States Department of Agriculture) [Public domain], via Wikimedia Commons. 10–Bildagentur Zoonar GmbH. 11–juefraphoto. 12–schankz. 13–Gabor Tinz. 14–TwilightArtPictures. 15–kzww. 16–B Calkins. 17l–blackeagleEMJ 17r – blackeagleEMJ. 18 – sasimoto. 19 – TinnaPong. 20 – kzww. 21 – https://commons.wikimedia.org/wiki/Category:Lineus_longissimus#/media/File:Nemertean_Lineus_longissimus.tif. 22 – schankz, Milosz_G. 23 – Graham Shaw, Madlen
Images are courtesy of Shutterstock.com. With thanks to Getty Images, Thinkstock Photo and iStockphoto.

CONTENTS

Words that look like **this** can be found in the glossary on page 24.

WHAT IS A WORM?

Worm

A worm is an animal with a long body, but no legs or **skeleton**. Worms live in the ground and eat dead plants.

Many worms like to live under the ground in damp soil. These worms are called earthworms. Earthworms live all over the world.

There are over 2,000 **species** of earthworm.

WHAT DO WORMS LOOK LIKE?

Earthworms usually grow to seven or eight centimetres long. Their bodies are pink or brown and are made of many ring-like **segments**.

Worms have a thicker ring near their heads. This makes a slimy substance that helps them move.

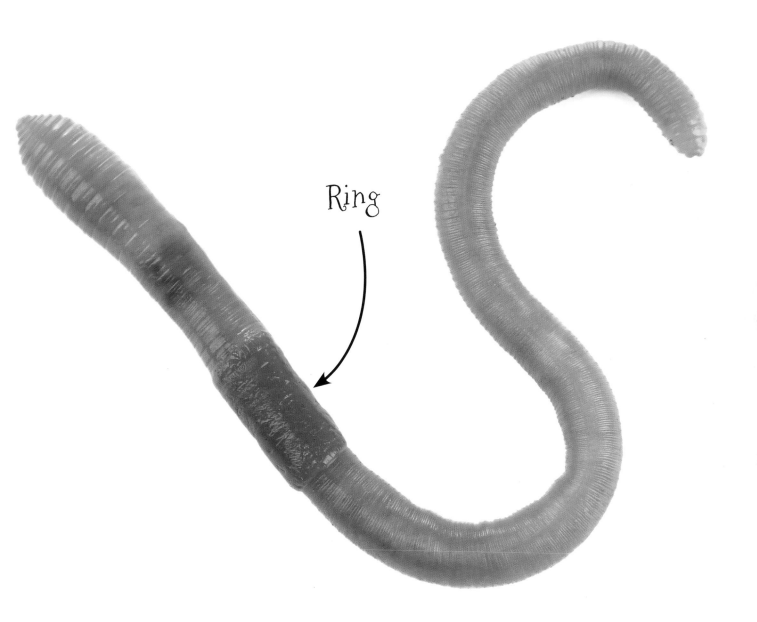

Ring

HOW DO WORMS LAY EGGS?

Worms are neither male or female, so they can all lay eggs!

When a worm lays an egg, it makes extra slime. This slime passes over the worm's body and covers the egg.

The slime forms a **cocoon** around the egg, which keeps it safe. These cocoons are smaller than a grain of rice.

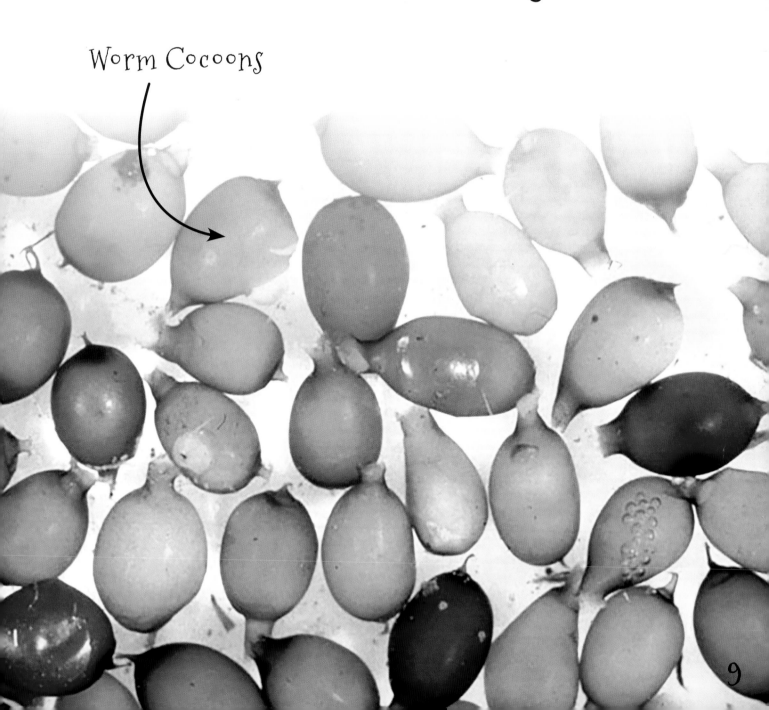

Worm Cocoons

WORM COCOONS

The cocoons usually take about three weeks to hatch. However, if the weather is too cold or the soil is too dry, the cocoons might stay unhatched for a lot longer. This protects them from the bad weather.

Worm cocoons can even survive being eaten by other animals! If eaten, they will come out in the animal's poo but will still be able to hatch.

One cocoon can be home to 20 eggs!

WHERE DO WORMS LIVE?

Earthworms live in tunnels that they make in the soil.
In the winter, they **burrow** deeper underground where
it's warmer.

Some people have a container in their garden full of old food and dead plants for worms to live in. This is called a wormery.

Wormery

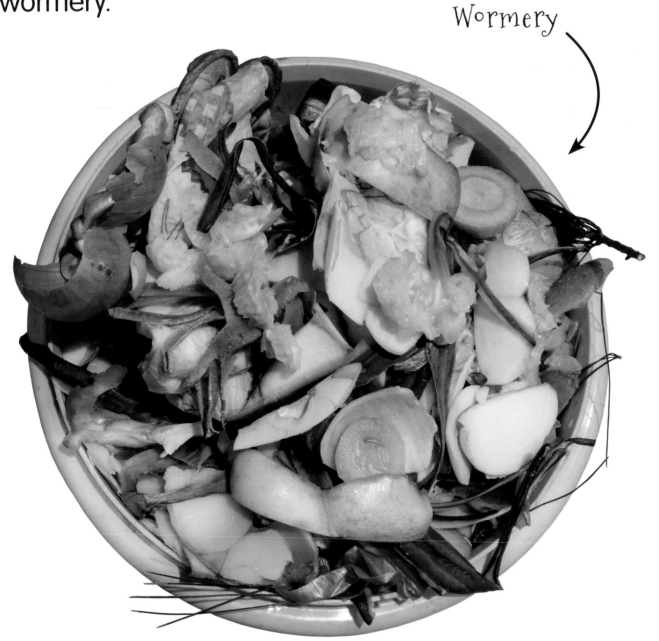

WHAT DO WORMS EAT?

Worms are not fussy eaters! They will eat anything from fruit and vegetables to dead plants and animals. They eat whatever they come across as they wriggle along.

Worms don't have teeth so they can't chew food. Instead, they eat small stones and grains of sand, which helps to grind up the food once it reaches the worm's **stomach**.

WHAT DO WORMS DO?

Earthworms spend a lot of time looking for food. When it rains, worms come out of the ground. This is because the water helps them to move quicker, making it easier to find food.

Seagulls are known for hunting worms by tapping the ground with their feet to make it sound like it's raining. When a worm appears, the gull will quickly grab it with its beak.

HOW DO WORMS HELP?

In one acre of soil there might be as many as one million worms.

Worms break down the **nutrients** in the food they eat.
These nutrients come out in the worm's castings.
A casting is another word for a worm's poo.

The nutrients in a worm's castings go back into the soil. This makes the soil more **fertile**, meaning that it will be easier for plants to grow in it.

WIGGLY WORMS

There are many species of worm in the world and some are very strange indeed! If you've ever been to the beach, you might have seen small, squiggly piles of sand. These are left behind by lugworms, which live under the sand on beaches.

Some worms live in the sea. The bootlace worm is the longest species of worm. The longest bootlace worm ever found was over 55 metres long.

Bootlace Worm

FUN FACTS

Worms breathe through their skin! The slime that covers their bodies helps them do this.

If worms are cut in two, the worm's head can survive and grow a new tail.

Some people take part in competitions to see who can get the most worms to come out of the ground. This is called worm charming.

Worms can eat half their body weight in food every day.

23

GLOSSARY

burrow	to make a hole or tunnel
cocoon	a protective shell that contains the worm's eggs
fertile	able to produce lots of plants and crops
nutrients	natural substances that plants and animals need to grow and stay healthy
segments	the individual rings that make up a worm's body
skeleton	the frame of bones that supports a body
species	a group of very similar animals or plants that are capable of producing young together
stomach	the part of the body where food is digested

INDEX